Teach me more... ENGLISH

by
Judy Mahoney

Learn English the fun way!

teach me... TAPES inc.

ISBN 0-934633-66-5

Printed in the United States of America

10 9 8 7 6 5 4 3 2

MARIE: Hello. My name is Marie. This is my brother. His name is Peter. We have a dog. His name is Spot. We have a cat. Her name is Fluffy. Follow us through the year.

You'll Sing a Song
You'll sing a song and I'll sing a song, and we'll sing a song together.
You'll sing a song and I'll sing a song, in warm or wintry weather.

PETER: It is spring. I plant a flower garden. Look at my white and yellow daisies!

MARIE: I plant seeds to grow fruit and vegetables in my garden. This year, I will grow strawberries, tomatoes, carrots, cabbage and pumpkins.

Oats and Beans and Barley

Oats and beans and barley grow,
Oats and beans and barley grow.
Do you or I or anyone know
How oats and beans and barley grow?

(Complete verses appear on page 16)

White Coral Bells

White coral bells upon a slender stalk.
Lilies of the valley deck our garden walk.
Oh, don't you wish,
That you could hear them ring?
That can happen only when the fairies sing.

APRIL

Going to the Zoo

Momma's taking us to the zoo tomorrow,
Zoo tomorrow, zoo tomorrow
Momma's taking us to the zoo tomorrow,
We can stay all day.
Chorus:
We're going to the zoo, zoo, zoo
How about you, you, you?
You can come too, too, too
We're going to the zoo, zoo, zoo.

Look at all the monkeys swingin' in the trees...
Look at all the crocodiles swimmin' in the water...

MARIE: Today we will go to the zoo. Look at the lion, the giraffe and the monkey.

PETER: My favorite animal at the zoo is the crocodile.

Tingalayo

Tingalayo, come little donkey come.
Tingalayo, come little donkey come.
Me donkey fast, me donkey slow,
Me donkey come and me donkey go.
Me donkey fast, me donkey slow,
Me donkey come and me donkey go.

(Complete verses appear on page 16.)

MARIE: My birthday is May 10. I have a party with my friends. My mother bakes me a big, round cake.

PETER: OK. Now it's time to play "Simon Says!"

Happy Birthday

Happy birthday to you!
Happy birthday to you!
Happy birthday, dear Marie,
Happy birthday to you!

"Simon Says"

Simon says: ... "put your right hand on
      your head."
... "touch the ground."
... "walk."
... "clap your hands."
... "say your name."
"Laugh out loud." "Simon didn't say!"

PETER: After spring, it is summer. In the summer, we go to the beach. I bring my beach ball and toy boat.

MARIE: I bring my sand pail and shovel to the beach.

PETER: We put on our swimsuits and build huge castles in the sand.

MARIE: Spot, don't knock it down!

Sailing, Sailing

Sailing, sailing,
Over the bounding main
For many a stormy wind shall blow
'Til Jack comes home again.

Row, Row, Row Your Boat

Row, row, row your boat
Gently down the stream
Merrily, merrily, merrily, merrily
Life is but a dream.

Down by the Seashore

Down by the seashore
Watch the little sea gulls
As they waddle down the beach
All in a row.

Down by the seashore
See the little tug boats
Pulling all the oil tankers
All in a row.

© Teach Me Tapes, Inc. 1994

(Complete verses appear on page 17)

5 FIVE

MARIE: After we swim, we eat our picnic lunch. We eat peanut butter sandwiches, cheese, carrots and bananas. It is delicious!

PETER: Oh no! Look at the ants!

MARIE: After our picnic, we go for a walk.

The Things of the Ocean

Little drops of water
Little grains of sand
Make the mighty ocean
So beautiful and grand.

Little bubbles floating
Little snails that slide
Make the mighty ocean
So beautiful and grand.

Every fish and coral
Every bird and clam
Make the mighty ocean
So beautiful and grand.

Every weed and turtle
Every whale and crab
Make the mighty ocean
So beautiful and grand.

Gentle dolphins swimming
Gentle rolling waves
Make the mighty ocean
So beautiful and grand.

Gentle gliding pelicans
A gentle seal at rest
Make the mighty ocean
So beautiful and grand.

(Complete verses appear on page 17)

MARIE: Today, we go to the natural history museum.
PETER: It is my favorite place because there are so many dinosaurs. Look at the triceratops. It has three horns on its head.

MARIE: Next, we go across the street to visit the art musuem.

PETER: I like to look at the bulls in Goya's painting. I pretend I am the matador.

MARIE: Look at the painting by Van Gogh. The flowers in his painting look like the ones in my garden.

Brown Girl in the Ring

Brown girl in the ring,
Tra-la-la-la-la (repeat)
She looks like a sugar
And a plum, plum, plum!

2. Show me a motion ...
3. Skip across the ocean ...
4. Do the locomotion ...

MARIE: After summer, it is autumn. The leaves turn gold, red and orange. We gather leaves and acorns that fall from the trees.

The Green Grass Grew

There was a tree
In all the woods,
The prettiest tree
That you ever did see.

The tree in the hole
And the hole in the ground,
The green grass grew all around, all around
And the green grass grew all around.

And on that tree ...
There was a limb ...

And on that limb ...
There was a branch ...

And on that branch ...
There was a twig ...

And on that twig ...
There was an acorn ...

(Complete verses appear on page 18)

PETER: Before we go back to school, we visit Grandpa's farm. We feed the cows, chickens and pigs.

MARIE: Grandpa shears the wool from the sheep. Later, he takes us on a hayride with our cousins.

Baa Baa Black Sheep

Baa baa black sheep, have you any wool?
Yes sir, yes sir, three bags full.
One for my master and
One for my dame,
One for the little boy
Who lives down the lane.
Baa baa black sheep, have you any wool?
Yes sir, yes sir, three bags full.

Down on Grandpa's Farm

Oh, we're on our way, we're on our way
On our way to Grandpa's farm. (repeat)

Down on Grandpa's farm there is a big brown cow (repeat)
The cow, she makes a sound like this: Moo! (repeat)

... there is a little red hen (repeat)
The hen, she makes a sound like this: Cluck! Cluck! (repeat)

Old MacDonald

Old MacDonald had a farm, E I E I O
And on that farm he had a cow, E I E I O
With a moo, moo here,
And a moo, moo there
Here a moo, there a moo,
Everywhere a moo, moo
Old MacDonald had a farm, E I E I O

... had a chicken, cat, some sheep.

MARIE: Today, our parents take us to the fall festival. We bring the vegetables from our garden to be judged.

PETER: There are many rides for the children. I love to ride the merry-go-round.

11 ELEVEN

PETER: It is Halloween. I am carving a face on my pumpkin.
MARIE: Tonight, I will dress up in my Little Red Riding Hood costume and Spot will be the wolf. Peter will be a cowboy. Then we will go trick or treating with our friends.
PETER: After Halloween, it is November.

Five Little Pumpkins

Five little pumpkins sitting on a gate
First one said, "Oh my, it's getting late."
Second one said, "There are witches in the air."
Third one said, "But we don't care."
The fourth one said, "Let's run and run and run."
The fifth one said, "I'm ready for some fun."
"Oo-oo," went the wind, and out went the light,
And the five little pumpkins rolled out of sight.

PETER: Look, snow is falling. Let's go and play in the snow. We take our sleds and slide down the hill.

MARIE: Then we'll build a huge snowman. He has coal eyes, a carrot nose and a derby hat. He wears my mother's scarf.

Snowman Song

There's a friend of mine
You might know him, too
He wears a derby hat
He's real cool.

He has coal black eyes
An orange carrot nose
Two funny stick-like arms
And a snowy overcoat.

Have you guessed his name
Or do you need a clue?
You'll never see his face
In autumn, summer, spring.

©Teach Me Tapes, Inc. 1989

Silent Night

Silent night, holy night,
All is calm, all is bright.
'Round yon Virgin, Mother and child
Holy infant, so tender and mild,
Sleep in heavenly peace,
Sleep in heavenly peace.

MARIE: It is holiday time. We celebrate Christmas. We bake cookies and decorate our house. We sing special songs.
PETER: January first begins the new year. We have a party to celebrate on New Year's Eve.

America the Beautiful

Oh, beautiful for spacious skies.
For amber waves of grain.
For purple mountains majesty,
Above the fruited plain.

America, America,
God shed His grace on thee.
And crown thy good with brotherhood,
From sea to shining sea.

MARIE: In February, we celebrate the Mardi Gras carnival. It is fun. I like to catch candy at the parade. We wear costumes and sing and dance with our friends.

PETER: Now we know the months of the year. Do you? January, February, March, April, May, June, July, August, September, October, November, December. Good-bye!

SONGS & DIALOGUE

PAGE 1
You'll Sing a Song
You'll sing a song and I'll sing a song,
And we'll sing a song together.
You'll sing a song and I'll sing a song,
In warm or wintry weather.
Words and music by Ella Jenkins. ASCAP

MARIE: Hello. My name is Marie. This is my brother. His name is Peter. We have a dog. His name is Spot. We have a cat. Her name is Fluffy. Follow us through the year.

PAGE 2 MARCH
PETER: It is spring. I plant a flower garden. Look at my white and yellow daisies!
MARIE: I plant seeds to grow fruit and vegetables in my garden. This year, I will grow strawberries, tomatoes, carrots, cabbage and pumpkins.

Oats and Beans and Barley
Oats and beans and barley grow,
Oats and beans and barley grow.
Do you or I or anyone know
How oats and beans and barley grow?

First the farmer plants the seeds,
Stands up tall and takes his ease,
Stamps his feet and claps his hands
And turns around to view his land.

Then the farmer waters the ground,
Watches the sun shine all around,
Stamps his feet and claps his hands
And turns around to view his land.

White Coral Bells
White coral bells upon a slender stalk.
Lilies of the valley deck our garden walk.
Oh, don't you wish, that you could hear them ring?
That can happen only when the fairies sing.

PAGE 3 APRIL
MARIE: Today we will go to the zoo. Look at the lion, the giraffe and the monkey.
PETER: My favorite animal at the zoo is the crocodile.

Going to the Zoo
Momma's (Daddy's) taking us to the zoo tomorrow,
Zoo tomorrow, zoo tomorrow
Momma's (Daddy's) taking us to the zoo tomorrow,
We can stay all day.
Chorus:
We're going to the zoo, zoo, zoo
How about you, you, you?
You can come too, too, too
We're going to the zoo, zoo, zoo.

2. Look at all the monkeys swingin'* in the trees...
3. Look at all the crocodiles swimmin'** in the water...
Words & music by Tom Paxton. Copyright 1961, renewed 1989.
Cherry Lane Music Publishing Co., Inc.

*"swingin'" is slang for "swinging"
**"swimmin'" is slang for "swimming"

Tingalayo
Tingalayo, come little donkey come.
Tingalayo, come little donkey come.
Me donkey fast, me*** donkey slow,
Me donkey come and me donkey go.
Me donkey fast, me donkey slow,
Me donkey come and me donkey go.

Tingalayo, come little donkey come.
Tingalayo, come little donkey come.
Me donkey he, me donkey haw,
Me donkey sleep in a bed of straw.
Me donkey dance, me donkey sing,
Me donkey wearing a diamond ring.

***"Me" is slang for "my."

PAGE 4 MAY
Happy Birthday to You
Happy birthday to you!
Happy birthday to you!
Happy birthday, dear Marie,
Happy birthday to you!

MARIE: My birthday is May 10. I have a party with my friends. My mother bakes me a big, round cake.
PETER: OK. Now it's time to play "Simon Says!"

Simon Says Game
Simon says: ... "put your right hand on your head."
                 ... "touch the ground."
                 ... "walk."
                 ... "clap your hands."
                 ... "say your name."
                       "Marie, Peter, Jenny, Joey."
"Laugh out loud." "Simon didn't say!"

PAGE 5 JUNE
PETER: After spring, it is summer. In the summer, we go to the beach. I bring my beach ball and toy boat.
MARIE: I bring my sand pail and shovel to the beach.
PETER: We put on our swimsuits and build huge castles in the sand.
MARIE: Spot, don't knock it down!

Row, Row, Row Your Boat
Row, row, row your boat
Gently down the stream.
Merrily, merrily, merrily, merrily
Life is but a dream.

Sailing, Sailing
Sailing, sailing, over the bounding main
For many a stormy wind shall blow
'Til Jack comes home again.

Down by the Seashore
Down by the seashore
Watch the little sea gulls
As they waddle down the beach
All in a row.

Down by the seashore
See the little tug boats
Pulling all the oil tankers
All in a row.

Down by the seashore
See the little sailboats
As they glide across the waves
All in a row.

Down by the seashore
See the little girls
As they build their sand castles
All in a row.

Down by the seashore
See the little boys
As they race their toy boats
All in a row.

Down by the seashore
See the sun is setting
Watch the people as they leave
All in a row.
©Teach Me Tapes, Inc. 1994

PAGE 6 JULY
MARIE: After we swim, we eat our picnic lunch. We eat peanut butter sandwiches, cheese, carrots and bananas. It is delicious!
PETER: Oh no! Look at the ants!
MARIE: After our picnic, we go for a walk.

The Things of the Ocean
Little drops of water
Little grains of sand
Make the mighty ocean
So beautiful and grand.

Little bubbles floating
Little snails that slide
Make the mighty ocean
So beautiful and grand.

Every fish and coral
Every bird and clam
Make the mighty ocean
So beautiful and grand.

Every weed and turtle
Every whale and crab
Make the mighty ocean
So beautiful and grand.

Gentle dolphins swimming
Gentle rolling waves
Make the mighty ocean
So beautiful and grand.

Gentle gliding pelicans
A gentle seal at rest
Make the mighty ocean
So beautiful and grand.

All the tiny sea shells
All the tiny bugs
Make the mighty ocean
So beautiful and grand.

All the tiny treasures
On the tiny islands
Make the mighty ocean
So beautiful and grand.
©Teach Me Tapes, Inc. 1994

PAGE 7 AUGUST
MARIE Today, we go to the natural history museum.
PETER: It is my favorite place because there are so many dinosaurs. Look at the triceratops. It has three horns on its head.

PAGE 8 AUGUST
MARIE: Next, we go across the street to visit the art museum.
PETER: I like to look at the bulls in Goya's painting. I pretend I am the matador.
MARIE: Look at the painting by Van Gogh. The flowers in his painting look like the ones in my garden.

Brown Girl in the Ring
Brown girl in the ring,
Tra-la-la-la-la (repeat)
She looks like a sugar
And a plum, plum, plum!

2. Show me a motion...
3. Skip across the ocean...
4. Do the locomotion...

PAGE 9 SEPTEMBER
MARIE: After summer, it is autumn. The leaves turn gold, red and orange. We gather leaves and acorns that fall from the trees.

The Green Grass Grew

There was a tree
In all the woods,
The prettiest tree
That you ever did see.

The tree in the hole
And the hole in the ground,
The green grass grew all around, all around
And the green grass grew all around.

And on that tree ...
There was a limb ...

And on that limb ...
There was a branch ...

And on that branch ...
There was a twig ...

And on that twig ...
There was an acorn ...

And by that acorn ...
There was a leaf ...

The leaf by the acorn
And the acorn on the twig
And the twig on the branch
And the branch on the limb
And the limb on the tree
And the tree in the hole
And the hole in the ground,
The green grass grew all around, all around
And the green grass grew all around.

PAGE 10 OCTOBER

PETER: Before we go back to school, we visit Grandpa's farm. We feed the cows, chickens and pigs.
MARIE: Grandpa shears the wool from the sheep. Later, he takes us on a hayride with our cousins.

Down on Grandpa's Farm

Oh, we're on our way, we're on our way
On our way to Grandpa's farm. (repeat)
Down on Grandpa's farm there is a big brown cow
(repeat)
The cow, she makes a sound like this: Moo! (repeat)

... there is a little red hen (repeat)
   The hen, she makes a sound like this: Cluck! Cluck!
(repeat)

Baa Baa Black Sheep

Baa baa black sheep, have you any wool?
Yes sir, yes sir, three bags full.
One for my master and
One for my dame,
One for the little boy who lives down the lane.
Baa baa black sheep, have you any wool?
Yes sir, yes sir, three bags full.

Old MacDonald

Old MacDonald had a farm, E I E I O
And on that farm he had a cow, E I E I O
With a moo, moo here and a moo, moo there
Here a moo, there a moo, everywhere a moo, moo
Old Mac Donald had a farm, E I E I O.

... had a chicken, cat, some sheep.

PAGE 11 OCTOBER

MARIE: Today our parents take us to the fall festival. We bring the vegetables from our garden to be judged.
PETER: There are many rides for the children. I love to ride the merry-go-round.

PAGE 12 OCTOBER AND NOVEMBER

PETER: It is Halloween. I am carving a face on my pumpkin.
MARIE: Tonight, I will dress up in my Little Red Riding Hood costume and Spot will be the wolf. Peter will be a cowboy. Then we will go trick or treating with our friends.
PETER: After Halloween, it is November.

Five Little Pumpkins

Five little pumpkins sitting on a gate
First one said, "Oh my, it's getting late."
Second one said, "There are witches in the air."
Third one said, "But we don't care."
The fourth one said, "Let's run and run and run."
The fifth one said, "I'm ready for some fun."
"Oo-oo," went the wind, and out went the light,
And the five little pumpkins rolled out of sight.

PAGE 13 DECEMBER

PETER: Look, snow is falling. Let's go and play in the snow. We take our sleds and slide down the hill.
MARIE: Then we'll build a huge snowman. He has coal eyes, a carrot nose and a derby hat. He wears my mother's scarf.

Snowman Song

There's a friend of mine
You might know him, too
He wears a derby hat
He's real cool.

He has coal black eyes
An orange carrot nose
Two funny stick-like arms
And a snowy overcoat.

Have you guessed his name
Or do you need a clue?
You'll never see his face
In autumn, summer, spring.

Who is it?
Can you guess?
C'mon, guess!
C'mon, don't you know?
It's the snowman!

Silent Night
Silent night, holy night,
All is clam, all is bright.
'Round yon Virgin, Mother and Child,
Holy infant so tender and mild,
Sleep in heavenly peace,
Sleep in heavenly peace.

PAGE 14 DECEMBER AND JANUARY
*MARIE: It is holiday time. We celebrate Christmas.
We bake cookies and decorate our house. We sing
special songs.
PETER: January first begins the new year. We have a
party to celebrate on Hew Year's Eve.*

America the Beautiful
Oh, beautiful for spacious skies.
For amber waves of grain.
For purple mountains majesty,
Above the fruited plain.
America, America,
God shed his grace on thee.
And crown thy good with brotherhood,
from sea to shining sea.

PAGE 15 FEBRUARY
*MARIE: In February, we celebrate the Mardi Gras
carnival. It is fun. I like to catch candy at the parade.
We wear costumes and sing and dance with our
friends.
PETER: Now we know the months of the year. Do
you?*

*January, February, March, April, May, June, July,
August, September, October, November, December.*

Good-bye!

Posters and additional learning materials are
available: 800-456-4656 or 612-933-8086

©Teach Me Tapes, Inc. 1994, 1997
  9900 Bren Road East, Suite B1-100
  Minnetonka, MN 55343-9664